D1162302

F/A-18 Hornet

F/A-18 Hornet

Roy Braybrook

Published in 1991 by Osprey Publishing Limited, 59 Grosvenor Street, London W1X 9DA

ISBN 1–85532–151–3

Edited by Tony Holmes
Designed by Paul Kime
Printed in Hong Kong

Front cover A trio of Hornets from Marine Air Group (MAG) 70 form up behind a VMGR-152 KC-130, another Hercules tanker from the same unit completing the 'leatherneck' formation. Photographed over the Persian Gulf in November 1990, the Hornets are from VMFA-314 'Black Knights' and VMFA-235 'Death Angels', both units being heavily involved in the bombing campaign of *Operation Desert Storm*. Both of the VMFA-314 aircraft are A-models whilst the singleton from VMFA-235 is a much newer C-model (*Yves Debay*)

Back cover The '43' on the funnel denotes that this is the 64,000 ton USS *Coral Sea*, a *Midway*-class carrier commissioned in October 1947. Completed too late for World War 2, these were the largest carriers of their day. They have a maximum speed of 32 knots (59 km/hr) and a range of more than 12,000 nm (22,000 km). They have a crew of 4560, and are powered by four Westinghouse steam turbines, giving a combined total of 212,000 shp. This photograph was taken in early 1986, with a VFA-132 'Privateers' FA-18A joined at the catapults by Hornet No 406 from the Marines' VMFA-323 *'Death Rattlers'* (*Angelo Romano*)

Half title page Two Canadian Forces CF-188s (serial 188703 in the foreground), photographed in late 1988. Both bear on their fin-tips the toned-down cougar's head insignia of No 410 Sqn, the operational training squadron, based at Cold Lake in Alberta (*Peter R Foster*)

Title page Hornets of Marine Corps squadron VMFA-314 'Black Knights', pictured over the Pacific Ocean near the coast of southern California. This unit was one of four Hornet squadrons that flew defence suppression missions against Libyan targets from the USS *Coral Sea* (CV-43) in 1986 (*Frank B Mormillo*)

Contents

Right Photographed on 20 October 1983, this F/A-18A (BuNo 161 710) was one of the first Hornets delivered to VFA-113 'Stingers' earlier that year. Along with sister-squadron VFA-25 'Fist of the Fleet', the 'Stingers' made history in 1985 when they participated in USS *Constellation's* (CV-64) WestPac, the first Pacific cruise for the Hornet. Part of the Fiscal Year 1981 buy of 60 aircraft, this Hornet wears the early McDonnell Douglas paint scheme of light compass ghost grey (Federal Standard 36375) on the upper surfaces and much lighter FS 36495 underneath (*Milslides via Bob Archer*)

302
VFA-113

West Coast Warriors

The McDonnell Douglas F/A-18 Hornet is the modern equivalent of World War 2's Vought F4U Corsair, the 'bent-wing bird' that racked up a kill ratio of 11 to one against Japanese fighters and was still flying close support missions for the USMC in the Korean War. Aside from the fact that both aircraft excel (or excelled) in terms of operational flexibility, they also have in common a somewhat undistinguished start. When the first unit equipped with the F4U-1 performed carrier trials on board the USS *Saratoga* (CV-3, not CV-60) in September 1942, the aircraft was criticized so much for its poor forward visibility and high landing speed that it was judged unsuitable for carrier operations, and was handed over to the Marines for land-based use. Likewise, the Northrop YF-17, from which the F/A-18 was derived, lost out to the General Dynamics YF-16 in a 1974 USAF contest for a new lightweight air combat fighter. It was only in the following year, when Congress directed the US Navy to consider navalized versions of the YF-16 and YF-17 as a means to replace both the A-7E and F-4J, that the twin-engined design came out on top. McDonnell Douglas (assisted by Northrop) then began the task of transforming a lightweight dogfight aircraft into a carrier-capable multi-role fighter with more than double the maximum take-off weight.

The first of an 11-aircraft FSD (Full-Scale Development) batch (including two two-seaters) bore the Bureau Number (BuNo) 160775 and had its maiden flight on 18 November 1978. This batch was originally to have been followed by 1366 production Hornets for 24 attack and six fighter squadrons for the US Navy and 12 fighter squadrons for the Marines. However, economy measures have since brought the total buy down to 1157 production aircraft, including 354 for the USMC and 48 modified for reconnaissance duties, to replace the RF-4B. In FY79 an initial batch of nine Hornets was ordered (Bu Nos 161213-17 and 248–251), followed by 25 in FY80 (161353–367 and 519–528), and 60 in FY81 (161702–761).

Sea trials began aboard the *Kitty Hawk* class *USS America* (CV-66) in November 1979, and a second series took place on the nuclear-powered *Nimitz*-class *USS Carl Vinson* (CVN-70) in April 1982. Initial deliveries were spread between two test establishments, VX-4 at Point Mugu and VX-5 at

Left This F/A-18A of VFA-113 'Stingers' typifies the highly toned-down markings of the Hornet in US Navy service, the hornet squadron badge and 'NK' tail-code of CVW-14 being barely visible. The unit transitioned from the A-7E (when it was VA-113) to the F/A-18 in 1983, and is home-based at NAS Lemoore. The squadron regularly cruised with CVW-14 aboard *Constellation* throughout the 1980s until the carrier went east for a Service Life Extension Program (SLEP) in early 1990 after completing another WestPac. Still with CVW-14, VFA-113 now operate off the smaller deck of USS *Independence* (CV-62), the 'Stingers' first WestPac aboard '*Indy*' seeing the squadron flying *Desert Shield* support missions in the later half of 1990 (*Frank B Mormillo*)

China Lake, and the Hornet Fleet Readiness Squadron, VFA-125 at NAS Lemoore, which initially provided training for both Navy and Marine pilots. More recently, training units have been established to deal separately with East Coast and Marine pilots, hence VFA-125 'Rough Raiders' is now primarily concerned with supporting the Pacific Fleets, i.e. the 3rd Fleet in the Eastern Pacific and the 7th Fleet in the Western Pacific and Indian Ocean. F/A-18 Hornet Squadrons assigned to the Pacific Fleet are as follows–

VFA-22	'Fighting Redcocks'
VFA-25	'Fist of the Fleet'
VFA-27	'Chargers'
VFA-94	'Mighty Shrikes'
VFA-97	'Warhawks'
VFA-113	'Stingers'
VFA-125	'Rough Raiders'
VFA-146	'Blue Diamonds'
VFA-147	'Argonauts'
VFA-151	'Vigilantes'
VFA-192	'World Famous Golden Dragons'
VFA-195	'Dambusters'
VFA-303	'Golden Hawks'
VFA-305	'Lobos'

Of these units, VFA-151, -192 and -195 are forward-deployed at NAF Atsugi in Japan as part of CVW-5 (tail-code 'NF'), and make cruises aboard the venerable USS *Midway* (CV-41), which is home-ported at Yokosuka. The remaining units are based at Lemoore, except for VFA-305 who call NAS Point Mugu home. It may also be noted that this squadron, along with VFA-303, are reserve units within CVWR-30; that VFA-132 'Privateers' was initially based at Lemoore before moving to the East Coast; and that VFA-161 'Chargers' was converting from the F-4 to the F/A-18 at Lemoore in 1986-87 when it was disbanded as an economy measure.

Aside from the various squadrons discussed above, smaller numbers of Hornets are also to be found in the West Coast area at NASA Ames/Dryden Flight Research Center at Edwards AFB, California; the Naval Weapons Center (NWC) at NAS China Lake, California; the Pacific Missile Test Center (PMTC) at Point Mugu, California; and the Naval Strike Warfare Center (NSWC) at NAS Fallon, Nevada.

Below This rare hangar photograph of one of VFA-125's Hornets illustrates the neat cockpit access ladder, which hinges down from the leading edge extension, the multi-lug wing-fold, and the far aft location of the main wheels, which was arranged to provide stability when the aircraft was being towed backwards on a rolling, pitching deck (*Tony Holmes*)

Right One of VFA-125's F/A-18s on tow, showing its remarkably wide-track undercarriage and drooping ailerons, giving much the same effect as full-span flaps (*Tony Holmes*)

GPC1

LT COL GRAY HUTCHINSON
EXECUTIVE OFFICER
"THUD"
WARNING
140
140
C
5

Left Pilots for the Pacific Fleets (and some USMC pilots) are trained by the Fleet Readiness Squadron (FRS) VFA-125 'Rough Raiders' at NAS Lemoore. Seen refuelling at the 'hot pits', this Hornet illustrates the Navy practice of stencilling the pilot's name where the Air Force would advertise the crew chief, and the pilot's use of a camouflaged bone-dome cover. This confirms that 'Thud' is a Marine, a fact borne out by his rank (*Tony Holmes*)

Above A sample of VFA-125 instructors, pictured in 1988, and representing (from left to right) the USMC, USAF, USN, CAF and RAAF. Spanish pilot training was carried out at Whiteman AFB in Missouri (*Tony Holmes*)

537

Left An action landing shot of a VFA-125 F/A-18B, bearing the 'NJ' tail-code for training aircraft based at Lemoore, Miramar, Whidbey Island and North Island (*Tony Holmes*)

Above Portrait of 'Thud's' transportation, bearing the '502' Modex, which is repeated on the trailing edge flaps to assist in launch identification, and in abbreviated form (02) on the fin. The standard droptank takes 275 Imp gal (1250 litres) of fuel, and the Hornet can carry three (*Tony Holmes*)

Hornet '564' on the deck of an unnamed carrier in 1988, in company with an E-2C early warning aircraft from VAW-110 'Firebirds', based at NAS Miramar. Along with VFA-125, VAW-110 are a West Coast training unit, both squadrons embarking aboard ship to give 'nugget' pilots their first taste of operations on a mobile deck (*Angelo Romano*)

Close-up of the leading edge extension (LEX) of a VFA-125 Hornet. The fence assists directional stability, reduces distortion in the engine airflow at high AOA, and throws a vortex over the wing that increases lift and delays flow separations. In the case of the original YF-17, Northrop placed a slot between the LEX and the fuselage to allow the boundary layer to be sucked away ahead of the intakes, but MDC closed the slot to reduce drag. The small fence has been added to modify the LEX vortex and reduce loads on the vertical tails, thus extending their fatigue lives (*Angelo Romano*)

Below An F/A-18B from VFA-125 releases two Mk 83 low drag bombs in a moderate dive attack over the live ranges at NAS Fallon. The course at Lemoore includes basic fighter manoeuvres and weapon training and ends with carrier qualification on the type. Students arrive with as little as 250 hours of previous experience, having flown only the T-34C, T-2J and TA-4J. The full six-month Hornet conversion course includes 90 flights and 113 flying hours, the first four sorties being flown dual, using the F/A-18B. The unit has approximately 16 F/A-18A/Cs and 24 F/A-18B/Ds, the two types averaging 45–50 and 55–60 hours per month respectively. The squadron's Hornets fly around 1700 hours monthly, this relatively high utilization reflecting the use of 'hot' refuelling, with up to six flights performed without stopping the engines. A new class of about 15 aviators begins the course at three monthly intervals, hence the output is around 60 qualified Hornet pilots each year (*MDC via Angelo Romano*)

Left The Hornet makes its Farnborough debut in 1980. The aircraft was serialled 160784, the 10th of the 11-ship development batch. At the time the two-seater was designated TF-18A, but this was later changed to F/A-18B. This aircraft was lost shortly after the show, following disintegration of the low-pressure turbine disc of the right engine, which also damaged that on the left. Construction of the disc was subsequently changed to eliminate this problem (*T Malcolm English*)

313
RESCUE
300

Left Line-up of VFA-303 'Golden Hawks' Hornets at NAS Lemoore in 1988. This was the first Reserve unit to receive the F/A-18. Prior to 1984 this was an A-7 unit (VA-303), based at NAS Alameda in California. The squadron then moved to NAS Lemoore, and received its first eight Hornets on 19 October 1985. Part of the West Coast Reserve Wing CVWR-30, its carrier deployments have included a 1988 cruise aboard the USS *Enterprise* (CVN-65) (*Tony Holmes*)

Above One of VFA-303's finest, illustrating the toned-down hawk insignia on the fin. As will be obvious from this 1988 photograph, the camouflage scheme applied to the F/A-18 has varied over the years. It is now estimated that the US Navy is flying Hornets with five or six different paint schemes, although they are all basically grey, and more recently with blue-grey markings. Although undoubtedly excellent for medium and high level air-to-air work, at low level the Hornet's pale grey would make it stand out like a sore thumb to any opposing fighter searching from a higher level. Nor are these camouflage schemes pleasing aesthetically – some of the examples illustrated later in this book are reminiscent of old zinc bathtubs! (*Tony Holmes*)

A six-ship formation combining aircraft from CVWR-30's two Hornet squadrons: VFA-303 'Golden Hawks' and VFA-305 'Lobos'. They were photographed in 1988 over the Mojave Desert in southern California, during a *Lobo Flag* exercise (*Frank B Mormillo*)

303
VFA-303

Left Pictured over the Pacific in 1987, a F/A-18A from VFA-305 (foreground) and one from VFA-303 (rear) maintain a loose formation. The squadron badge for '305 is even more toned-down than the hawk of '303. It takes the form of a wolf's head ('*lobo*' being Spanish for wolf) in a circle within a triangular shape. When painted on the aircraft the wolf is heading forwards, but in the case of the formal insignia it is looking to the right, backed by a green and white sash over the legend 'STRKFITRON 305' (*Frank B Mormillo*)

Below Illustrating the high contrast provided by a light grey against a blue sea, VFA-303's No 303 is pictured somewhere over the Pacific. Note the non-slip walkway added over the LEX (*Frank B Mormillo*)

503
503
503

Left A pleasing shot of VFA-305's No 503, this Modex standing out clearly on the nose and trailing edge flap. The virtually unswept wing of the Hornet is a reflection of Northrop design philosophy that large sweep angles are undesirable because the ailerons lose their effectiveness. A straight wing clearly penalizes acceleration times and maximum speed (that for the F/A-18 is a modest 'Mach 1.7 plus'), but it proved to be a godsend in developing a carrier-based aircraft with a slow approach speed. It also means that in a traditional type of dogfight, with aircraft losing energy and ending up low and slow, the Hornet retains better controllability than almost any other aircraft in its class (*Frank B Mormillo*)

Above Flaps down, No 503 closes in on the photographer standing on the open cargo ramp of the KC-130. For readers who like details, the Hercules came from the Marine Reserve unit VMGR-352, which is based at MCAS El Toro in California and carries the tail-code 'QB' on its KC-130F/Rs (*Frank B Mormillo*)

Above Side-view of VFA-305's No 505. Strangely, this aircraft carries the full Modex on the fin and only the last two digits on the front fuselage.
(Frank B Mormillo)

Right Closer still, and we can see the white helmet of a Navy pilot, and such details as the external brackets added to the base of the vertical tail units. Note also the way in which the gases from the M61 Vulcan gun are released sideways, presumably to minimize deposits on the windscreen. Although night firings must blind the pilot, the Hornet has one of the finest gun installations ever designed, in the sense that the M61 fires approximately through the aircraft CG, and thus produces neither pitch nor yaw. Complete with 570 rounds, a storage drum (which also accepts the empty cases after firing), and a linkless feed system, the gun system weighs 841 lbs (381 kgs). It is removed from the aircraft as a complete unit, downwards through the gun-bay door. The Hornet can be loaded with ammunition in a radhaz environment and at a rate of 400 rounds/min, using GE's LALS (linkless ammunition loading system)
(Frank B Mormillo)

Above Another member of VFA-305, in this case No 507, approaches the tanker. The first digit of the Modex is unchanged throughout the squadron, and the '00' aircraft ('500' in the case of VFA-305) is usually that of the commander air group (CAG). The '01' and '02' designations are reserved for the aircraft of the squadron commander and executive officer, but higher numbers have no special significance (*Frank B Mormillo*)

Above right 'Lobo' No 505, as seen in 1989 over the practice ranges at NAS Fallon, Nevada. The BuNo appears to be 161755, which would place it as one of a batch of 60 F/A-18s purchased by the US Navy in FY81 (*Frank B Mormillo*)

Below right This excellent photograph of No 507 firing 5-inch (127 mm) Zuni rockets over the ranges at NAS Fallon was a joint effort in which Frank B Mormillo set up the camera, and Lt Cdr Pat O'Rourke tripped the shutter. One rocket can clearly be seen emerging from the pod, while its flame is still exhausting from the far end (*Lt Cdr Pat O'Rourke USN*)

505
505

507
507

An assembly of grey Hornets on the ramp at NAS Fallon during CVWR-30's annual two-week training programme, involving aircraft from both VFA-303 and -305. Note the rocket launcher and adaptor on the pylon of the F/A-18 in the foreground. During the det in July 1989 both units flew a combined total of 250 flight hours in 405 sorties over the 'live' ranges at Fallon, VFA-303 winning the loft delivery and strafing competition and VFA-305 taking the overall honours as the most accurate bombing unit in CVWR-30 (*Frank B Mormillo*)

02
05
504
503
301

207
VFA-151
NF
MIDWAY

103

Above left Hornet BuNo 162908 of VFA-151 'Vigilantes', landing at Kadena, Okinawa, in 1988. The aircraft bears the '207' Modex and the 'NF' tail-code for CVW-5, which generally operates from the USS *Midway* (CV-41), the name of which appears on the rear fuselage. This unit was formerly VF-151, equipped with the F-4S. It was, in fact, the first Phantom II squadron to transition to the Hornet, the new designation being applied on 17 June 1986. The unit is forward-deployed at NAF Atsugi in Japan, near the *Midway*'s base at Yokosuka on the main island of Honshu. The squadron badge is a skull and three elliptical orbits in a darker circle (*Bob Archer*)

Below left Another component of CVW-5 based at Atsugi is VFA-195 'Dambusters', instanced here by No 103. Formerly an A-7E squadron, it was redesignated on 1 April 1985, converted to the Hornet, and was reassigned to Japan on 10 November 1986. The unit badge appears to take the form of the head of a screaming eagle. Note that 'VFA-195' is painted on the fin, rather than the fuselage (*Tony Holmes*)

Above A quartet of Hornets from VX-5 attack aircraft evaluation squadron, tail-code 'XE', aboard the *Forrestal*-class *USS Ranger* (CV-61) in late 1982. As with other Navy aircraft based at China Lake, VX-5 'Vampires' Hornets now carry on their fins the Naval Weapons Center insignia, which combines an eagle with an anchor and two guided missiles (*MDC via Angelo Romano*)

22
9410
VS-41
34

A Hornet of VX-5, about to be launched from *Ranger*. As with all other modern carrier-based aircraft, the F/A-18 is catapulted by means of a nosewheel tow system. In this photograph the tie-bar on the noseleg has been lowered to engage with the shuttle of the steam catapult, and the massive actuator that will shortly retract the leg forwards is ready to transfer the catapult loads into the centre fuselage. The aircraft in the background is a Lockheed S-3A Viking, BuNo 159410, from VS-41 'Shamrocks', based at NAS North Island California, and wearing the same 'NJ' tail-code as the Lemoore-based Hornet training squadron VFA-125 (*MDC via Angelo Romano*)

Above Armament specialists from VX-5, preparing 80-series bombs for an F/A-18 aboard *Ranger*. These low-drag free-fall bombs were developed in the early postwar period for the US Navy, using shapes designed by Douglas Aircraft, replacing wartime bombs that were much blunter, to suit internal carriage. Retarded ('Snakeye') versions came later. Note also the complexity of the wing articulation, and the unusual shape of the Hornet pylons, which support the bomb well forward (roughly abreast of the aircraft CG), but have to be cut back to clear the leading edge flap *(MDC via Angelo Romano)*

Right White knuckle time! A 'Vampire' pilot prepares to be hurled into the inky blackness with a Hornet strapped to his back. Night-time carrier operations are almost certainly the most dangerous form of peacetime flying, but the F/A-18 is the safest tactical carrier aircraft in the history of naval aviation. In the first half-million flight hours with the USN and USMC, 22 Hornets were lost, compared to 50 F-14s, 63 A-6s, 95 F-4s, 111 A-7s and 144 A-4s. The dim red lighting of the flight deck area protects the pilots' night vision, and the circles showing up on the deck are simply lash-down points (*MDC via Angelo Romano*)

28
VX-5
NAVY

Below A Hornet attached to VX-4 'Evaluators' fighter test and evaluation squadron (tail-code XF) in flight over the Pacific Missile Test Center at NAS Point Mugu, California. The marked nose-down incidence of the Sidewinder mountings is intended to eliminate the tendency for upwash around the stores to stall the wingtips prematurely (Frank B Mormillo)

Left This Sparrow-armed F/A-18 was photographed in 1982, while assigned to the VX-5 attack aircraft evaluation squadron (tail-code XE) at NAS China Lake *(Frank B Mormillo)*

The Cecil 'Nest'

Hornet test, evaluation and training units on the West Coast may have taken precedence in deliveries, but East Coast squadrons were first to see operational use. A training squadron to support the 2nd Fleet in the Atlantic and the 6th Fleet in the Mediterranean was established at NAS Cecil Field in Florida in April 1984 (three years after Lemoore) as VFA-106 'Gladiators'.

The Hornet's first chance for action came in March 1986 when, following terrorist strikes at Rome and Vienna airports, the US severed links with Libya, and President Reagan authorized *Operation Prairie Fire*. This involved sending elements of the 6th Fleet into the Gulf of Sirte, crossing Colonel Gaddafi's 'Line of Death' at latitude 32°30′ N in the process. One of the carriers involved was the veteran *Midway* class carrier USS *Coral Sea* (CV-43). This was the first class designed from the outset to operate jet fighters, but it was physically too small to operate the F-14. Instead, the *Coral Sea* had on board 48 Hornets forming four squadrons: VFA-131 and -132, and Marine units VMFA-314 and -323. In the various clashes with Libya, these F/A-18s were required to use both their fighter and attack capabilities, fending off Mirages, Su-22s, and MiG-23s and -25s that came too close, and later carrying out low level defence suppression strikes against the SA-5 SAM (surface-to-air missile) site at Sirte, using the brand-new Texas Instruments AGM-88A HARM (High-speed Anti-Radiation Missile).

Given evidence that the 5 April 1986 terrorist attack on a West Berlin nightclub was only the first of a planned series of Libyan-inspired strikes against US citizens and facilities, President Reagan authorized *Operation El Dorado Canyon* to further demonstrate to Gaddafi that sponsoring terrorism was a punishable offence. Three targets in the Tripoli area, including the military side of the international airport, and two at Benghazi (one of which was Benina airfield), were to be attacked simultaneously on 14 April, which required carrier-based assets to be augmented by USAF aircraft operating from the UK. The Hornet's role again was defence suppression (in

Right Two Hornets from VFA-15 'Valions' combine to provide side and plan-views of the aircraft, and an illustration of a fairly recent paint scheme, with little variation in colour over the airframe. The unit bears its rampant lion insignia in off-white form, rather than the usual darker grey. Formerly VA-15, equipped with the A-7E, it was redesignated in October 1986, but remained at NAS Cecil Field. In the photograph the tail-code is the 'AC' of CVW-3, which was earlier associated with USS *Saratoga* (CV-60) but recently has been assigned to USS *John F Kennedy* (CV-67). The Hornets of VFA-15 now bear the 'AJ' code of CVW-8, and with this wing sailed on the initial operational cruise of the *Nimitz*-class carrier USS *Theodore Roosevelt* (CVN-71). Specialists at 'breaking in' new carriers, VFA-15 and CVW-8 also participated in the initial shakedown of the navy's newest carrier, USS *Abraham Lincoln* (CVN-72), in January 1990 (*MDC via Angelo Romano*)

VFA-15
303
VALIONS

conjunction with A-7Es), and the F/A-18s fired a total of 30 AGM-88As against SAM sites. They were fired on by SA-2s, SA-3s, SA-6s and SA-8s, but returned to the *Coral Sea* without loss.

Aside from the Fleet Replacement Unit VFA-106, the following squadrons are assigned to the East Coast–

VFA-15	'Valions'	VFA-131	'Wildcats'
VFA-81	'Sunliners'	VFA-132	'Privateers'
VFA-82	'Marauders'	VFA-136	'Knight Hawks'
VFA-83	'Rampagers'	VFA-137	'Kestrels'
VFA-86	'Sidewinders'	VFA-203	'Blue Dolphins'
VFA-87	'Golden Warriors'		

In addition, VFA-37, -46, -72, and -105 are due to receive Hornets at Cecil Field in the course of 1991, as are the reservists at VFA-204 in New Orleans. Aside from the squadrons listed above, smaller numbers of Hornets are to be found at the Naval Air Test Center (NATC) at NAS Patuxent River.

Below The boss of the 'Valions' comes over the blunt end of CVN-71 in No 300, groping for a wire. During the 1989 cruise aboard the 'TR', the 'Valions', along with the remainder of CVW-8, operated with the French Navy in the Mediterranean during *Exercise Phinia '89* (*Jean-Pierre Montbazet*)

Right Hook down, VFA-15's No 311 is about to land on the *Theodore Roosevelt* in early 1989. The three drop-tanks and the practice bomb carrier on the port outer pylon indicate an air-to-surface operation over a distant range. It may be added that the term 'landing' is one of many misused words in aviation English. The French, who made an earlier start in aviation, and provided words such as '*fuselage*' and '*empennae*', also have more precision in describing a return to earth. Aside from the basic '*atterrissage*', they have '*appontissage*' for a deck landing and '*amerissage*' for alighting on water (*Jean-Pierre Montbazet*)

VALIONS

200
VFA-15
VALIONS
307

VF-84
201
VFA-15
300

Above left No 307 taxies clear of the landing area, its wing fold reducing the span from 40.7 to 27.5 ft (12.4 to 8.4 m). Despite the toned-down markings, the squadron has still managed to add some colour to the leading edge and twin fins of the 'Hornet'. The Tomcat in the background is more brightly coloured because it is the CAG-bird of VF-84 'Jolly Rogers', the aircraft flown by the commander of the wing. The aircraft's black fins bear the squadron's skull-and-crossbones insignia (*Jean-Pierre Montbazet*)

Below left A meeting of CAG-birds on the waist cat. I wonder which aircraft the 'boss' is flying on this sortie!? The 'E' on the tail of the Tomcat indicates that the squadron has maintained a high level of combat readiness over a specified period of time (*Jean-Pierre Montbazet*)

Above The driver of VFA-15's No 305 applies full lock in heading for the starboard catapult (*Jean-Pierre Montbazet*)

400
CVW
17
NO PUSH
USS SARATOGA

Left This remarkable rear-end shot of Hornet serial 163477 indicates from the '400' Modex and CVW-17 badge that this aircraft is the CAG-bird for VFA-81 'Sunliners', the unit embarked aboard USS *Saratoga* (CV-60). The squadron was previously an A-7E unit (VA-81) based at Cecil Field, and was redesignated on 4 February 1988. When this photograph was taken in September 1988, the 'Sunliners' were still transitioning onto brand new F/A-18Cs in preparation for their first Mediterranean cruise with the re-born '*Super Sara*' in late 1988 (*Tony Holmes*)

Above A veritable flying arsenal, this F/A-18C No 314 from VFA-82 (serial 163465) is carrying eight Mk 83 bombs in addition to its centreline tank, two AIM-7 Sparrows and two AIM-9L Sidewinders. The windows under the front fuselage suggest that it has (at least) provisions to replace the gunpack with a reconnaissance package (*MDC via Angelo Romano*)

Left View from the bridge of the *Kitty Hawk*-class USS *America* (CV-66). In the foreground, the boss-man's Hornet from VFA-82 'Marauders'. Beyond, a miscellany of A-6s and S-3As, and a C-2A Greyhound about to be launched, the raised blast-fence protecting personnel and other aircraft from the propwash of its Allison T56 turboprops. As in the previous illustration, the Hornet is also that of the commander of the wing, and bears the CVW-1 insignia on its fin, rather than the sea-bird and trident badge of VFA-82. The squadron was previously an A-7E unit, and was redesignated on 15 July 1987. This was the first unit to receive the F/A-18C, which has provisions for the AIM-120 AMRAAM (Sparrow replacement), Maverick and ASPJ jammer (*Duncan Cubitt/Airforces Monthly*)

Above Number 307 with multi-role store configuration, including two Texas Instruments AGM-88A supersonic anti-radar missiles and centreline Rockeye, which is now marketed by Ferranti International as the Mk 7 cluster weapon (*MDC via Angelo Romano*)

Left Depicted in an optimistically vertical attitude, Hornet No 307 from VFA-82 illustrates the mixed store configuration employed by the 6th Fleet in its probing missions against Libya in early 1986. Its two AIM-9Ls and two AIM-7s allowed it to deal with any airborne opposition, while the two AGM-88A HARMs on the outer pylons could suppress enemy radars, and the centreline Rockeye cluster bomb unit (CBU) could sink a patrol boat. The M61 cannon could deal with a range of airborne and surface targets (*MDC via Angelo Romano*)

Above left These F/A-18Cs of VFA-82 demonstrate typical warloads for air-to-air and air-to-surface missions. Number 314 carries eight Mk 83 bombs, while retaining its two AIM-7s, two AIM-9s and M61 cannon. The CAG's aircraft ('300', serial 163467) has an additional four AIM-9s on the underwing pylons. Both carry a centreline tank. Note the squadron badge on the tail of '314', and the blue 'AB' and 'VFA-82' markings on the CAG-bird (*MDC via Angelo Romano*)

Above right This two-ship loop by Hornets from VFA-82 again emphasized operational versatility, the farther aircraft illustrating a possible defence suppression load of two AGM-88As and one CBU, and the near aircraft presenting an anti-shipping strike configuration, with two AGM-84 Harpoon sea-skimming missiles in addition to the basic air-to-air weapons.

405
VFA-86
405

Above left Hornet No 407 represents VFA-86 'Sidewinders', which (like VFA-82) is based at Cecil Field and assigned to CVW-1 (tail-code 'AB') on board the *America*, where this photograph was taken in 1990 (*Duncan Cubitt/Airforces Monthly*)

Below left A steamy shot of VFA-86's No 405, preparing for the catapult. Note the small bulges around the front fuselage, which are believed to house the ASPJ antennas, and provide the only external means to distinguish an F/A-18C from the basic A-model (*Duncan Cubitt/Airforces Monthly*)

Above No 405 departs CV-66, showing its drooped ailerons and toed-in rudders. Since the Northrop YF-17 was designed for land-based operations, the F/A-18 is much higher off the deck than an aircraft such as the A-7, which was designed from the outset for stability on a highly mobile deck. As a result, the mainwheels of the Hornet have been placed so far aft that it is difficult to rotate the aircraft in a shore-base take-off. For this reason the rudders are toed inwards during take-off, to create drag that will help to pull the nosewheel off the ground. In carrier take-offs rotation is no problem, but the rudders are toed in regardless (*Duncan Cubitt/Airforces Monthly*)

AJ
VFA-87
405
624

Left A crowded parking area on the deck of the USS *Theodore Roosevelt*. Beyond the EA-6B of VAQ-138 and the A-6E of VA-35, are a mixture of F/A-18s from VFA-87 'Golden Warriors' and VFA-15, distinguished by their squadron insignia: a Red Indian warrior's head and a rampant lion, respectively (*Jean-Pierre Montbazet*)

Above Hornet No 406 waits for a catapult shot, while the Intruder is prepared to go. The latter's BuNo (152912) comes from one of the batches of A-6As that were converted to KA-6D tankers, the total number converted being 192 (*Jean-Pierre Montbazet*)

Above Any landing you can walk away from is a successful landing. VFA-87's No 401 taxies away from a successful deck landing on the *Roosevelt* in early 1989
(*Jean-Pierre Montbazet*)

Right Looks like someone was trying for a cover-shot for some magazine! This wide-angle view of VFA-87's No 405 in the final stage of the approach depicts the Hornet with everything down
(*Jean-Pierre Montbazet*)

Right We only use afterburner if there is a TV crew on deck!' VFA-87's No 401 goes off the deep end at military power, sinking slightly (*Jean-Pierre Montbazet*)

Below Love the shades, but keep working on the moustache! 'Golden Warriors' pilot, call-sign 'Shortney', prepared to go over the sharp end of CVN-71, sandwiched between his Martin-Baker SJU-5/6 and his Kaiser AVQ-28 HUD (*Jean-Pierre Montbazet*)

401
401

Left If there is any doubt in the mind of this student pilot from VFA-106, the guy in the foreground obviously thinks that he should go thataway, and the character on the right is either a 'peacenik', or is trying to say that both pieces of machinery seem to be turning. VFA-106 'Gladiators' was formed as the East Coast Fleet Readiness Squadron at NAS Cecil Field, Florida, on 27 April 1984 (*Angelo Romano*)

Above On foreign soil, a Hornet (BuNo 163099) of VFA-87 is seen taxying in at RAF Abingdon in September 1988, with typical British 1960s housing in the background (*Robbie Shaw*)

300
AD
VFA-106

352
331
AD
VFA-106

Above left Very obviously the boss-man's machine, this F/A-18D (BuNo 163454) carries the '300' Modex, the 'AD' tail-code for aircraft shore-based at Cecil Field, Oceana or Key West, and the unit's gladiator and spear insignia in coloured form. The picture was taken at NAS Cecil Field in May 1990 (*Robbie Shaw*)

Left In contrast to the previous illustration, this F/A-18D (BuNo 163445, No 352) is just another twin-holer on VFA-106's books, hence the squadron badge in toned-down form (*Robbie Shaw*)

Above Pictured in a neat six-ship formation whilst on detachment to NAS Fallon for weapons training, these Hornets of VFA-131 'Wildcats' wear their insignia in toned-down form. The unit was originally established at Lemoore in October 1983, but transferred to Cecil Field in February 1985. Bearing the 'AK' tail-code of CVW-13, it made several cruises on the USS *Coral Sea* (including the *Prairie Fire* operation against Libya in 1986), before being assigned to CVW-17 (tail-code 'AA') aboard USS *Independence* (CV-62) and subsequently CVW-7 (tail-code 'AG') aboard USS *Dwight D Eisenhower* (CVN-69)
(*MDC via Angelo Romano*)

Above Photographed on the deck of CVN-69 during a visit to Portsmouth in 1990, this Hornet (BuNo 162394) bears the '410' Modex and the 'AG' code of CVW-7. To the right can be seen the tail of A-6E, BuNo 161231, with the '500' Modex and winged skull insignia of VA-34 'Blue Blasters' (*Peter R Foster*)

Right Seen on the deck of the *Coral Sea* in early 1986 just before the altercation with Libya, this member of VFA-131 wears the 'AK' code of CVW-13 and a store carrier capable of lifting any number of practice bombs. Those at the front presumably duplicate the behaviour of the free-fall Mk 80-series, whereas the blunt store further aft may represent a Snakeye retarded bomb (*Angelo Romano*)

USS CORAL

NEXT PM
0207

Left A nosewheel-tow launch means two wheels and twice as many nosewheel tyres to check. Nonetheless, maintenance man-hours per flight hour (MMH/FH) are running at 27.6 for the F/A-18, compared to 43.5 for the A-7E, 57.0 for the A-6E and 63.8 for the F-14A. Mean flight hours between failures (MFHBF) stand at 1.9 for the Hornet, compared to 0.8 for the A-7E, 0.6 for the A-6E and 0.5 for the F-14A (*Tony Holmes*)

Above VFA-131's No 105 is firmly attached to the catapult shuttle, and is about to depart from the CV-43 in early 1986, while the boss-man's aeroplane from VMFA-323 'Death Rattlers' waits its turn, wings folded (*Angelo Romano*)

Below The tail-feathers of Hornet BuNo 162452, as painted when VFA-131 was assigned to CVW-7 aboard the CVN-69. The markings are notably more visible than in the unit's *Coral Sea* days (*Angelo Romano*)

Right As seen at NAS Cecil Field in 1990, the smartly decorated CAG-Hornet of VFA-132 'Privateers', bearing the 'AK' code for CVW-13, which (as indicated by the classy writing) was normally embarked aboard the now-decommissioned *Coral Sea*. The serial number is 162422 and the Modex '200'. In the past the squadron insignia has appeared as a pirate's head, but in this instance it has been changed to a galleon and two aircraft (*Robbie Shaw*)

200
Coral Sea
VFA 132
NAVY
CVW 13
200

Left All Hornets look as though they have just experienced a very heavy landing, but that splayed-out appearance was the only way to achieve a satisfactory undercarriage track. Note the black anti-dazzle area and walkways, which are somewhat unusual (*Zone Five*)

Above 'Privateer' No 204 in flight with one Sidewinder and one ACMI data pod. Whereas the CAG's aircraft has the galleon in white, in this case it appears to be blue-grey. The unit was established at Lemoore in January 1984, and was one of the four Hornet units aboard the old CV-43 during the cruise that lasted from October 1985 to May 1986 and included the two operations against Libya. The unit was next forward deployed to MCAS Iwakuni in Japan to support the 1st Marine Air Wing, a detachment that lasted from October 1987 to May 1988. It subsequently rejoined CVW-13 and the *Coral Sea* with the 6th Fleet in the Mediterranean (*Paul F Crickmore*)

204
AK
NAVY
206
VFA 132

Left Number 206 moves up into echelon port on No 204 as the 'loose deuce' cruise down the Florida coastline from NAS Cecil Field to NAS Key West (*Zone Five*)

Above So the hook works, but has he forgotten the landing gear? This flashback to early 1986 shows 'Privateer' No 206 in toned-down markings and with the old squadron badge, showing a pirate with large hat and obligatory eye-patch (*Via Angelo Romano*)

TOP
CAUTION
NO LIFT
VFA 136
Little Giant Ladders

Left Accessibility has been designed into the Hornet, as illustrated by this photograph of an aircraft from VFA-136 'Knight Hawks'. For radar access the radome is swung round to starboard and the Hughes APG-65 can then be run forward on tracks. The 20 mm General Electric M61 Vulcan gun is mounted on a pallet, complete with ammunition tank and feed system, and is located immediately behind the radar. For access the gun bay door in the bottom of the fuselage is opened and the complete cannon package can then be lowered to a cradle on the deck (*Angelo Romano*)

Above Formerly an A-7E unit (VA-203), VFA-203 'Blue Dolphins' is one of the most recent squadrons to receive the Hornet. This photograph was taken in 1990 at NAS Cecil Field (code 'AF'), the F/A-18A (BuNo 161951) being the mount of CVWR-30's CAG (*Robbie Shaw*)

Marine Muscle

As indicated earlier, USMC pilots were initially trained by VFA-125 at NAS Lemoore. The first operational Hornet unit was, in fact, the Marine Corps squadron VMFA-314, which trained there between July and December of 1982, and reached operational status at MCAS El Toro in California on 7 January 1983. This unit was later joined by VMFA-323 and -531, to form Marine Air Group (MAG) 11 of the 3rd Marine Air Wing (MAW), which is tasked with providing air support for the 1st Marine Expeditionary Force (MEF). In the same way, MAG 31 of the 2nd MAW at MCAS Beaufort, South Carolina, supports the 2nd MEF, and MAG 24 of the 1st MAW at MCAS Kaneohe Bay, Hawaii, supports the 3rd MEF. Active duty VMFAs completed their conversion from the F-4 to the F/A-18 during Fiscal Year 1989, and the Reserve units will convert in the early 1990s. In this latter context, the 4th MAW will swap two F-4, one F/A-18 and five A-4 squadrons for five F/A-18 and two AV-8B squadrons.

Aside from the Marines' training unit, VMFAT-101 (tail-code 'SH'), the following squadrons are believed to be operational with the USMC–

VMFA-115	'Silver Eagles'	VMFA-312	'Checkertails'
VMFA-122	'Crusaders'	VMFA-314	'Black Nights'
VMFA-134	'Hawks' (Reserves)	VMFA-323	'Death Rattlers'
VMFA-212	'Lancers'	VMFA-333	'Shamrocks'
VMFA-232	'Red Devils'	VMFA-451	'Warlords'
VMFA-235	'Death Angels'	VMFA-531	'Gray Ghosts'
VMFA-251	'Thunderbolts'		

In addition, the two-seat F/A-18D is now replacing the Marines' A-6E Intruder in the day/night all-weather attack role, and will in future replace the OA-4 and RF-4 in observation and reconnaissance missions. The first such unit is VMFA(AW)-121 'Green Knights', and reports suggest that this will be followed by -202, -224, -242, -332 and -533. It is also reported that the Hornet will equip VMFA(AW)-225 'Vagabonds' in the reconnaissance role, replacing the recently retired RF-4Bs of VMFP-3 'Eyes of the Corps', and the F-4s and A-4s of VMFA-321, -142, -112 and -322 of the Marine Corps Reserve.

Left Not the sexiest-looking aeroplane ever designed, the Hornet looks really sick with that trailing-link main-gear dragging along somewhere behind the aircraft. This F/A-18A (BuNo 163155) is from VMFA-115 'Silver Eagles' (code 'VE') bearing an '03' Modex. Formerly an F-4S unit, VMFA-115 transitioned onto the Hornet at MCAS Beaufort in 1985. Part of MAG-31, the unit has forward deployed to MCAS Iwakuni, in Japan, and participated in *Exercise Northern Wedding* from Vandel in Denmark over the past five years. Wearing the '03' Modex on its nose, this Hornet was photographed on recovery to NAS Oceana, Virginia, in April 1989 (*Peter R Foster*)

VE
VE
VMFA-115
MARINES

VE
VMFA-115
MARINES

Above left Marine Hornet units are often as well travelled as their Navy cousins, this VMFA-115 FA-18A basking in the warm morning sun at Royal Australian Air Force (RAAF) base Pearce, in Western Australia. Part of a large Corps detachment to the 'sunny southern climes' for *Exercise Valiant Usher '87*, BuNo 162464 was one of ten 'Silver Eagles' that forward deployed from Iwakuni specially for the 'invasion' of Western Australia (*Tony Holmes*)

Below left Photographed at MCAS Beaufort (pronounced 'Biewfort' in May 1990, this F/A-18A (BuNo 162458) carries the 'VE' code of VMFA-115 and the '05' Modex (*Robbie Shaw*)

Above Another resident of MCAS Beaufort as part of MAG-31 is this Hornet, BuNo 161977, which wears the 'DW' code of VMFA-251 'Thunderbolts', the unit's highly distinctive tail insignia, and the '07' Modex. Previously an F-4S unit with the same designation, VMFA-251 converted to the F/A-18 in 1986. Note the furtive carriage of the 'DW' code on the inboard fin surfaces (*Robbie Shaw*)

VMFA-314
VMFA-314
VMFA-314
01
08
VW
MARINE

Below This strange diamond formation provides a useful beginners' test for aircraft enthusiasts. The photograph was taken at MCAS Cherry Point (aka Cunningham Field) in North Carolina in April 1989. The lead aircraft is an A-6E bearing the BuNo 159573 and the 'EA' tail-code of VMA(AW)-332 'Polka Dots'. The trail aircraft is an F/A-18 with the 'DR' code of VMFA-312 'Checkertails', which converted from the F-4S in early 1988. The wing aircraft are an OA-4M bearing the 'DA' code of the Headquarters & Maintenance Squadron (H&MS-32) and an AV-8B from VMA-542, which bears the 'WH' code (*Peter R Foster*)

Left A three-ship formation from VMFA-314 'Black Knights'. This squadron is distinguished by its 'VW' code, the insignia being reduced to a knight's helmet on the centre fuselage, between the 'VMFA' and the '314' (*Frank B Mormillo*)

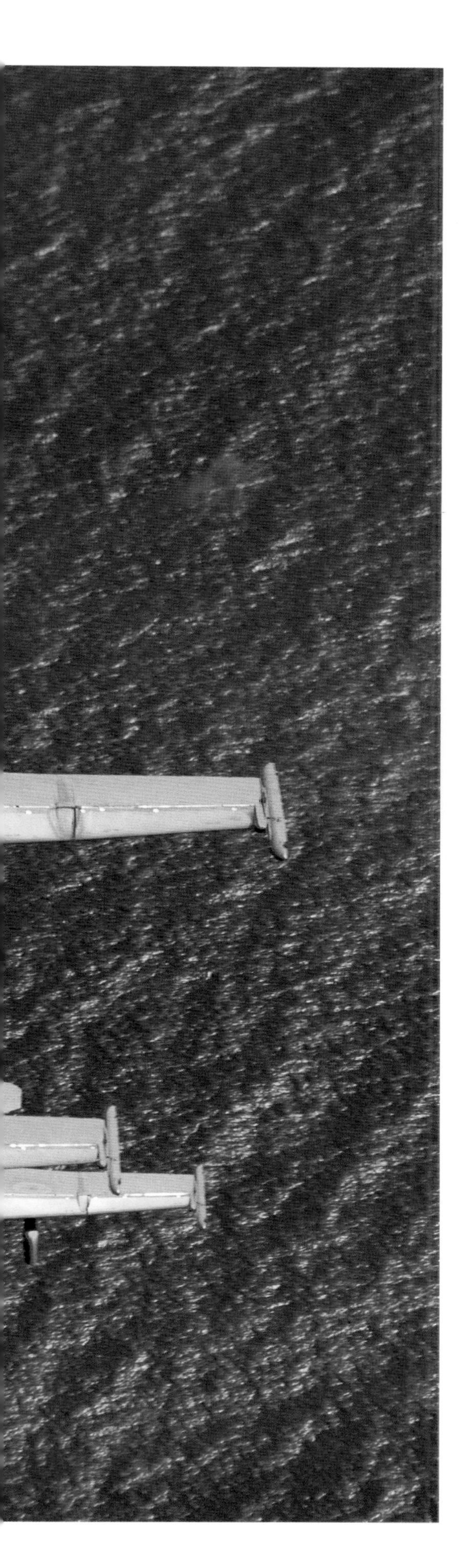

Above Head-on view of a VMFA-314 F/A-18A, hook down. The 'Black Knights' were heavily involved in anti-armour strikes against Iraqi tanks in Kuwait during *Operation Desert Storm*, thus proving the true versatility of the Hornet (*Yves Debay*)

Left The Blue Angels aren't going to lose any sleep over this outfit! The 'Black Knights' began their conversion at NAS Lemoore in August 1982 and were declared operational in January 1983. This was one of the units involved in the conflict with Libya in 1986, when it was operating from the *Coral Sea*. It was subsequently deployed to Egypt for *Exercise Bright Star '87*, and was based for six months at Iwakuni in Japan. The squadron is currently based at MCAS El Toro, California as part of MAG-11 (*Frank B Mormillo*)

Above An interesting example of VMFA-314's late-1990 markings. Cruising at height over the Persian Gulf, this aircraft appears in long-range air defence configuration with four Sparrows, two Sidewinders and three external tanks. As the aircraft was performing an operational patrol when this photo was taken, all the missiles visible in this shot are live, hence the yellow stripes (*Yves Debay*)

Right Four Marine Corps Hornets stepped down in line-astern with an out-of-place KC-130. The first two F/A-18s hail from VMFA-314, but the last two of the stack are from VMFA-235 'Death Angels'. The latter unit (tail-code DB) is based at Marine Corps Air Station Kaneohe Bay, Hawaii where it forms part of MAG-24. This unit transitioned from the F-4S to the F/A-18 at El Toro in 1989, returning to the islands in September of that year (*Yves Debay*)

Above Coming over the back end of *Coral Sea*, 'Black Knight' No 304 has everything down, and the driver in the white helmet is hoping for a wire (*Angelo Romano*)

Above right The other Marine squadron aboard CV-43 at the time of the Libyan conflict was VMFA-323 '*Death Rattlers*', exemplified here by the CAG's aircraft, bearing the '400' Modex. This unit also went with VMFA-314 to Egypt in 1987 for *Exercise Bright Star*, and spent six months at Iwakuni. It is likewise based at MCAS El Toro (*Angelo Romano*)

Below right Seen from a different angle, VMFA-323's No 410 prepares to depart from the *Coral Sea* in early 1986, while in the background a VFA-132 'Privateers' Hornet stands in line for the port catapult (*Angelo Romano*)

VMFA-323
400
AK

VMFA-323
410
AK
207
506
305

Below 'Death Rattlers' No 603 rapidly decelerates after snagging a three wire, its pilot feeling the G force in the cockpit as he strains on his harness straps. The VMFA-323 insignia takes the form of a band of diamonds at the top of the fin, an identification that also appeared on the squadron's F-4S (*Angelo Romano*)

Right Multi-role combat aircraft of two widely-separated generations, bearing the 'WS' code of VMFA-323, the F/A-18 goes nose-up to hold station with the F4U-1 Corsair from the 'Planes of Fame' collection, currently housed at Chino in California (*Frank B Mormillo*)

W S
80
80

VMFA-333
01

Pictured on the ramp at MCAS Beaufort in 1990, this Hornet carries the 'DN' code of VMFA-333 'Shamrocks' and that unit's distinctive emblem on the base of the fin. The 'OI' Modex denotes that it's the CO's aircraft (*Robbie Shaw*)

Above With the rudder suitably positioned, the third shamrock of the squadron insignia appears. The groundcrew are using a bomb-hoist to mount a FLIR-pod on the intake duct, in place of the AIM-7 missile. The Hughes AAR-50 FLIR or thermal imaging navigation set (TINS) provides the pilot with either a narrow (3 degree) or wide (12 degree) view of the outside world, and in the case of the Night Attack Hornet this can be projected on the HUD. A separate targeting FLIR can track targets in the air or on the ground *(Robbie Shaw)*

Above right The 'Shamrocks' No 08, BuNo 161979, at MCAS Beaufort in 1989. The unit converted to the Hornet in 1987, and for a time was forward deployed to Iwakuni, but is now part of MAG-31 at Beaufort *(Bob Archer)*

Below right More business for the tyre manufacturer, as 'DN/08' lands in a puff of smoke. Note the FLIR pod attached to the port Sparrow groove. The 'Shamrocks' previously operated the F-4S, and were based at MCAS El Toro on the West Coast *(Robbie Shaw)*

08
DN
VMFA-333
08

08
DN
08

Photographed on the ramp at MCAS Beaufort, this F/A-18A carries the 'VM' code of VMFA-541 'Warlords' and that unit's tail insignia and star-spangled band around the centre fuselage. The squadron previously flew the F-4S from the same base. Following conversion, the squadron deployed to Bodo in Norway in September 1988 for *Exercise Teamwork*. It then joined the *Coral Sea* (and thus adopted the 'AK' code of CVW-13) for the carrier's last cruise with the 6th Fleet in the Mediterranean in 1989 (*Robbie Shaw*)

Two bomb-laden Hornets from VMFA-451 formate neatly with Harpoon and Sparrow-armed Hornets from VMFA-312, which is coded 'DR' and named the 'Checkertails'. Note the yellow and red borders to the chequered stripe. Like the 'Warlords', VMFA-312 converted from the F-4S and is based at MCAS Beaufort (aka Merritt Field) in South Carolina (*MDC via Angelo Romano*)

Above Nice portrait of Hornet BuNo 162467 at MCAS El Toro, California. Its fin has the 'EC' code of VMFA-531 'Gray Ghosts', a unit that converted from the F-4N at Lemoore in 1983. The squadron insignia consists of a skull with two lightning bolts radiating from the ocular apertures (*Robbie Shaw*)

Right A pair of 'Gray Ghosts' on combat air patrol (CAP) over the Marine Corps Air-Ground Combat Center at Twenty nine Palms in California. This quaintly-named bush airfield is perhaps best known for the high risk of snake-bites to visiting personnel (*Frank B Mormillo*)

Above This rear-quarter view of 'EC/01' shows the unit badge more clearly on the fin, and in full colour on the hangar door (*Robbie Shaw*)

Right A member of VMFA-531 (foreground) joins up over the Pacific with a Canadian Hornet bearing the cougar insignia of No 410 Operational Training Unit, the latter aircraft appearing significantly darker than the USMC example (*Frank B Mormillo*)

VMFA-531
04

The ‘Blues’

The US Navy’s Blue Angels flight demonstration squadron is an important element of Naval Air Training Command, and was formed at NAS Corpus Christi in Texas in 1946. Since then this unit has operated 10 different types of aircraft, including the F-4 from 1969 to 1973, the A-4F from 1974 to 1986, and the F/A-18 from 1987. The selection of this latest aircraft began well before the end of the Skyhawks’ last display season, and the principal alternatives to the Hornet were the forthcoming T-45A Goshawk (another McDonnell Douglas product) and a Skyhawk that had gone through a SLEP (service life extension programme). The A-4Fs had been flown intensively (about 500 hr/yr) and three had been lost in accidents, hence additional aircraft would have to be modified to ensure adequate numbers. A further consideration was that the Blue Angels are intended to demonstrate to potential Navy pilots the aircraft that they can fly in the service. From that viewpoint there was little sense in extending the use of the obsolescent A-4, and there was a good case for the Hornet. The Goshawk would have been significantly less expensive to operate (and the example of Britain’s Red Arrows with its BAe Hawk forebear indicated that the aircraft would be well suited to the role), but it would be some years before examples would be available without disrupting the flight trials or its introduction into service.

On 25 February 1986 the US Navy consequently selected the F/A-18 to replace the A-4F in Blue Angels service. Eleven aircraft were to be converted (including two trainers) from an early production batch, Lot IV, corresponding to Hornets 17 to 28. These aircraft were not carrier-capable, but had been used primarily for pilot training from land bases, and were thus of limited value in an operational sense without a major upgrade. For use by the Blue Angels the principal modification was to remove the M61 gun and replace it with an oil injection system with a 67 Imp gal (303 litre) tank and a pump to inject the oil into the jets. In addition, the muzzle aperture was faired over, and the blast shield replaced by 258 lbs (117 kgs) of lead ballast. The fuel system was modified to provide for longer inverted flight, the seat harnesses were changed for the same reason, Collins VOR/ILS was added to facilitate the use of civil airports, and the old nickel-cadmium batteries were replaced by sealed lead-acid gel units. The first aircraft was modified at St Louis, but the remainder were processed at the Naval Air Rework Facility (NARF) at North Island, California. Finally, they were painted in blue and gold at their home base at NAS Pensacola, Florida.

Training began at their winter home at NAF El Centro, California in January 1987, and the first display was flown at MCAS Yuma, Arizona, on 25 April 1987. The team normally flies up to 80 displays each year. In the event of war, these non-standard aircraft would go to a Fleet Readiness Squadron for use in pilot training.

Right The US Navy’s ‘Blue Angels’ are perhaps not as imaginatively decorated as the USAF’s ‘Thunderbirds,’ but all the prime advertising space appears to have been sold. The aircraft on the left carries the serial 161524, indicating that it is one of a batch of 25 aircraft purchased in FY80, which was only the second year of production (*MDC via Angelo Romano*)

U.S.NAVY

Below The reflections in the wing testify to the glossy finish applied to this demonstration aircraft. Note also the 'Blue Angels' badge and the retention of Sidewinder rails, which (as in the cases of the F-5 and F-16) form permanent anti-flutter masses (*MDC via Angelo Romano*)

Right Fish-eye view from a centreline pod during a barrel roll. Although these early Hornets are not cleared for carrier operations, they all have arrestor hooks. The nearest aircraft wears BuNo 161527, making it another FY80 buy. One surprising detail is that the inlet duct is painted white, which is the latest fashion in reducing head-on 'black-dot' detectability (*MDC via Angelo Romano*)

161527
2
Blue Angels
U.S.NAVY
7
Blue Angels

More wide-angle work. The 'Blue Angels' are best known for their six-ship diamond formation, in which the aircraft are only 36 inches (90 cm) apart, with wings overlapping (*MDC via Angelo Romano*)

Hornets Abroad

The F/A-18 has not enjoyed the massive overseas sales of the F-16 or the Mirage or MiG families of fighters, but throughout the 1980s it has won consistently in the case of prosperous nations with a genuine need for multi-role capability.

The first contract came in April 1980, less than two years after the maiden flight of the F/A-18, and only months after the formation of the first US Navy training unit. Attracted by the idea of twin-engined safety in operations over the frozen north of its territory, Canada signed for a total of 138 Hornets, including 24 (later increased to 40) two-seaters. The contract included an option on a further 20 aircraft, but five years later Canada declined this option, citing a shortage of funds and a lower than expected attrition rate. The Canadian Hornet is known officially as the CF-188, and the first example bore the serial 188901. It first flew on 29 July 1982 and was handed over to the CAF (Canadian Armed Forces) three months later. The last delivery took place in September 1988. Hornets of the Canadian Forces are generally referred to as CF-18As and -18Bs. They equip the training unit, No 410 'Cougars' Sqn, three 16-aircraft squadrons in Germany (No 409 'Nighthawk', No 421 'Red Indian' and No 439 'Sabre-tooth Tiger') and four 12-aircraft squadrons in Canada (No 416 'Lynx', No 425 'Alouette', No 433 'Porcupine' and No 441 'Silver Fox'). The three units at CFB Baden–Söllingen were formerly referred to as 1 CAG, but this designation has now been replaced by No 4 (Fighter) Wing of No 1 Canadian Air Division. In war, this would be reinforced by No 3 (Fighter) Wing at Lahr, consisting of Nos 416 and 433 Sqns. At present Nos 410, 416 and 441 Sqns are based at CFB Cold Lake in Alberta, and Nos 425 and 433 Sqns at CFB Bagotville in Quebec. In late 1990 some 18 aircraft from No 409 Sqn were deployed from Germany to provide air cover for Canadian vessels involved in the Gulf crisis. Flown by pilots from all four Baden–Söllingen-based units, the Hornets flew many 'sweep and escort' missions after *Desert Storm* commenced. In view of the non-appearance of the Iraqi Air Force, the CF-18s were later switched to ground attack.

The second order came from Australia, with a contract signed in October 1981 for a total of 75 Hornets, including 18 two-seaters. In this case only the first two aircraft were completed at St Louis, the remainder being assembled in Melbourne by Aerospace Technologies of Australia, with the engines

Right This Canadian Forces CF-18A carries on its fin-tip the insignia of No 409 'Nighthawks' Sqn, which completed conversion in June 1985 and became the first unit of No 4 Wing at Baden–Söllingen. It was later joined by Nos 421 and 439 Sqns, and in the event of war in Europe would be supported by Nos 416 and 433 Sqns which would form No 3 Wing at Lahr. Note the fake cockpit painted under the front fuselage, to confuse opposing pilots regarding the attitude of the aircraft. Most air forces have concluded that this is too dangerous for peacetime use, though some would employ it in wartime (*Robbie Shaw*)

Photographed in early 1990, this Hornet comes from No 409 Sqn at Baden–Söllingen. The '752' on the front fuselage implies that the full serial is 188752, which puts it in the middle of the single-seat batch (188701–789). Serials for the CF-18B run from 188901 to '940 (*Robbie Shaw*)

provided by Hawker de Havilland Victoria and the radar by Philips in Sydney. The official designations are AF-18A and ATF-18A, but again these are rarely used. The first aircraft (serial A21-101) was handed over in St Louis on 29 October 1984, and the two US-assembled Hornets for the RAAF were ferried from NAS Lemoore to RAAF Base Williamtown, New South Wales, in May 1985. The first locally-assembled Hornet has its maiden flight on 26 February 1985, and deliveries were completed in May 1990. The RAAF Hornets form four units: No 2 OCU, and Nos 3 and 77 Sqns all at Williamtown; and No 75 Sqn at Tindal in the Northern Territory.

The third export order came from Spain, with a contract for 72 Hornets (including 12 two-seaters) signed in May 1983. In this case the manufacturer's designations are EF-18A and EF-18B, but the Spanish Air Force (*Ejercito del Aire*) refers to these aircraft as the C15 and CE15. These aircraft form *Escuadrónes* 121 and 122 of *Ala de Caza* (Fighter Wing) 12, and *Esc* 151 and 152 of *Ala* 15, with both wings initially based at Zaragoza, although the former wing was moved to Torrejon near Madrid in early 1989.

Another 'Nighthawk', in this case serial 188740, photographed on a visit to RAF Waddington for the Tactical Fighter Meet in 1988. It is equipped with an AIM-9 acquisition round and practice weapons pod (*T Malcolm English*)

Above Two CF-18As (serials 188709 and '760) break right. The fin badge is that of No 410 'Cougar' Tactical Fighter (Operational Training) Squadron, which was formed at Cold Lake in Alberta in June 1982. Initially, instructor training was performed in the US, but deliveries of Hornets to Cold Lake began in October that year, student training getting underway in January 1984. The OTU has a secondary air defence role within NORAD *(Peter R Foster)*

Right The cockpit of a No 410 Sqn Hornet. Its principal feature is the use of three large multi-function displays (cathode ray tubes), of which the central one is normally employed as a horizontal situation display (HSD). The other two are used to present mission data, radar and other sensor displays, maintenance data, weapons status, navigation information, etc. Combined with the advanced HUD, the up-front controller, and the grouping of essential controls on the throttles and stick, these displays give the Hornet what is probably the best cockpit of any contemporary fighter *(Ian Black)*

FUEL QTY
HOOK
WING FOLD
EMERG JETT
BINGO
HUD SYM
AOA INDEXER

ARMÉES

CANADA
188760

Above left Despite the advanced navigation system of this No 410 Sqn CF-18A, the pilot still finds it necessary to stow a few maps on the glare-shield. The Hornet conversion course involves 85 flight hours, plus 40 hours in the simulator and 200 hours of ground school. The 'Cougars' can trace their ancestry back to 1941, when they were formed in Scotland on the Boulton-Paul Defiant. They later flew the Beaufighter and Mosquito, but were disbanded in 1945. Reformed in Canada in 1948, No 410 flew the Vampire, then the Canadair-built CL-13 Sabre, the CF-100 Canuck and the CF-101 Voodoo. This photograph unfortunately omits the LEX strake, which in the case of 410 Sqn carries a leaping cougar (*Ian Black*)

Below left Pictured at low level over Bavaria in late 1988, CF-18A serial 188760 carries in barely visible form the Red Indian head and crossed tomahawks of No 421 'Red Indian' Sqn, which is now part of the No 4 (Fighter) Wing at Baden–Söllingen. The squadron reached operational status in June 1986 (*Peter R Foster*)

Above Two CF-18As overshoot Baden–Söllingen, with '760 in the lead. Although now seen only in microscopic toned-down form, the Red Indian insignia has been with No 421 Sqn for decades and on several types of fighter, including the Spitfire during World War 2, the CL-13 Sabre and the CF-104 Starfighter (*Peter R Foster*)

152-01
151-03

Below As seen at Zaragoza-Valenzuela in Northern Spain, this EF-18A wears the serial C15-45, and the unit designation 12–03 on the front fuselage, indicating that it is a member of No 12 Wing. The wing previously operated the F-4C and RF-4C, and reports indicate that, although Nos 121 and 122 Sqn have now equipped with the Hornet, No 124 retains eight RF-4Cs for tactical reconnaissance. The wing moved to Torrejon de Ardoz in early 1989. The Phantom II's of this wing carried a unit badge in the form of a dark blue wildcat's head in a white circle, but such an insignia is not immediately apparent on this EF-18A (*Robbie Shaw*)

Left The first four two-seat EF-18Bs in echelon port, with serials CE15-4, -3, -2, and -1 (front to rear) and corresponding squadron markings 152-04, -03, -02, and 151-01. The use of squadron markings such as these ceased in 1987, when they were superseded by wing codes such as the '12–03' of the preceding photograph. This change was probably encouraged by centralized servicing, which made it more convenient to allocate an aircraft temporarily to one squadron or another according to demands, rather than making a permanent assignment. The red and yellow roundel features colours dating back to the 12th Century Kingdom of Aragon, and has been in use on Spanish aircraft for more than 60 years. The black St Andrew's cross on a white ground was part of the Nationalist markings introduced in 1936 in the early days of the Spanish Civil War (*MDC via Angelo Romano*)

In giving the reasons for Australia's selection of the F/A-18, the Defence Minister emphasized the need for versatility and the ability to operate over the country's vast northern regions without the close control available in Europe. He also emphasized reliability in deployments to bare bases, the need to minimize peacetime training losses, and the potential to accommodate later weapons and equipment. This photograph of F/A-18s from No 2 Operational Conversion Unit was taken in May 1986, one year after the unit received its first Hornets. Note the carriage of practice weapon pods on two aircraft *(Greg Meggs)*

An F/A-18B on the ramp at RAAF Williamtown in August 1985, its well-smoked nose suggesting that the gun has been fired recently. This airfield is the principal fighter base in Australia, and is situated near Newcastle, just north of Sydney. Australian Hornets have the type designation A21 (the Mirage having been A3, and the F-111 A8), and this example is serialled A21-102. The serials run from A21-1 to -57 for the single-seaters and A21-101 to -118 for the two seaters. At time of writing only two have been lost in accidents: A21-104 struck Palm Island near Townsville on 18 November 1987 during a night bombing practice and A21-42 from No 75 Sqn crashed following a collision during ACM practice near Tindal on 2 August 1990, killing the squadron CO, Wing Commander Ross Fox (*Greg Meggs*)

Line-up of No 2 OCU Hornets at RAAF Townsville in Queensland, where they were based temporarily for bombing practice. The serials visible are A21-105, -102, -106, and -107. The arrestor hook has been retained, but the catapult tow-bar has been deleted. The only significant change from the basic US Navy standard F/A-18A/B is the addition of an HF radio. Minor changes include an Australian fatigue data analysis system (AFDAS), an improved video/voice recorder, the clearance of standard RAAF practice bombs, the addition of a landing light, the introduction of a Martin-Baker seat harness, and the use of ILS/VOR in place of the carrier landing system. In addition, 23 Australian Hornets have wiring provisions for the reconnaissance pod to replace the gun package in the front fuselage. As seen here, the No 2 OCU insignia consists of a black and yellow chevron and a tiger's head (*Greg Meggs*)

Hornet A21-08 of No 3 Sqn, seen at RAAF Pearce during the unit's first full deployment to the West Coast in March 1987. The flight refuelling probe is not often seen, since the RAAF has only recently taken delivery of its first tanker. Four 707 conversions have been funded, with ASTA in Melbourne installing flight refuelling kits purchased from Israel Aircraft Industries. The first delivery to the RAAF took place in July 1990. Prior to this, the only opportunity to practice in-flight refuelling was during joint exercises with US services. However, the two RAAF Hornets completed by MDC were ferried nonstop from NAS Lemoore to Williamtown in May 1985, with tanking provided by SAC KC-10s. The flight covered a distance of 6690 nms (12,390 kms) and took 15 hours (*Tony Holmes*)

Below Hornet A21-15, showing the Southern Cross insignia of No 3 Sqn. Prior to converting to the F/A-18 in 1986, this unit operated the Mirage IIIO in the air defence role at Butterworth in Malaysia. The RAAF had a permanent presence at the base from 1958 to May 1988, when No 79 Sqn was disbanded. However, that was not the final operational Mirage unit as No 75 Sqn at Darwin continued to operate for a short period. In place of the permanent basing of Mirages at Butterworth, from September 1988 Hornets have been detached to that base and Singapore for shorter periods totalling 16 weeks per year (*Tony Holmes*)

Right No 9 breaks away, its leading edge flaps depressing slightly and showing such details as the Sparrow grooves, the massive aileron actuator fairings, the area suction on the intake splitter plate and the far forward location of the centreline pylon. The RAAF fin flash remains similar to that used on Britain's RAF aircraft, but the kangaroo roundel was introduced shortly after World War 2. It may be noted that the 'roo always faces forwards and (on the wing) has his feet toward the tips. In addition to the national markings, RAAF F-111s also carry a small Australian flag at the top of the fin, but the embellishment is peculiar to that type (*Greg Meggs*)

A21-9

09
A21

A21-108

Above left Another member of No 3 Sqn, A21-9, pictured in flight over the Australian outback in June 1987. Note the fuselage stripe, and the stylized sword in the centre. Aside from detachments to Butterworth and Singapore, aircraft from No 3 Sqn have visited the RNZAF base at Ohakea on New Zealand's North Island in April 1987, and Clark AB in the Philippines later that year during *Exercise Cope Thunder* (*Greg Meggs*)

Below left It looks like another good day for a barbie as No 3 Sqn's A21-108 pulls alongside the photographic aircraft, leading edge flaps cracked down slightly. All three operational squadrons are required to have a multi-role capability, including the use of laser-guided bombs (LGBs) and the AGM-84 Harpoon sea-skimming anti-ship missile, but No 3 Sqn also has a special responsibility to develop air-to-air tactics (*Greg Meggs*)

Above A slightly unusual view of No 75 Sqn's A21-23, pictured at Darwin in the course of *Exercise Kangaroo '89*. The unit markings appear to be an inverted BOAC 'Speedbird' on the fin and a centre fuselage Kiwi 'Tiki' good luck symbol, sometimes referred to as a 'grumpy monkey'! The squadron is based at Tindal, which is less vulnerable to seaborne attack than Darwin, is outside the cyclone belt and is safe from salt water corrosion problems. On the other hand, this base is even less popular than Darwin as a posting, since it is about 60 kms from the coast and any sizeable population centre. Construction began decades ago, the original aim being to build a major airbase that could survive in a nuclear war, but it was completed in the late 1980s, to accept No 75 Sqn's Hornets in September 1988 (*Greg Meggs*)

Below Two Hornets of No 77 Sqn over the sea in region of Darwin. The unit is based at Williamtown, where it reformed on the F/A-18 in the second half of 1987, having previously been the Mirage OCU (*Greg Meggs*)

Right Another example of No 77 Sqn equipment, this time A21-29, seen taxiing at Darwin. The unit insignia consists of a chequer-board fin-stripe, top hat and cane, and a magpie badge on the centre fuselage (*Greg Meggs*)

29

Below This early (1988) photograph of a 77 Sqn aircraft (A21-27) shows it without the top hat and cane fin markings. Three Hornets from this squadron deployed with No 3 Sqn to Clark AB in late 1987 to participate in the *Cope Thunder* exercise (*Greg Meggs*)

Right Photographs of RAAF Tindal are extremely rare, presumably for security reasons, and this picture of a 77 Sqn Hornet (A21-45) provides a tantalising glimpse of an Australian hardened aircraft shelter. The gum trees in the background suggest that a certain amount of natural cover may also be available if reinforcing aircraft have to be parked in the open (*Greg Meggs*)

45
45

What is this man thinking? If both 'donks' (engines) stop, either the snakes or the sharks will get me? If it weren't for this ejection seat, I could actually see my six o'clock? If only Australia could have afforded the F-15? The fact is that Australia's selection of the Hornet proved once again that a reasonably prosperous nation with a real need for multi-role capability will generally select the F/A-18 (*Greg Meggs*)